# YOUR KNOWLEDGE HAS VALUE

**Bibliographic information published by the German National Library:**

The German National Library lists this publication in the National Bibliography; detailed bibliographic data are available on the Internet at http://dnb.dnb.de .

**Imprint:**

Copyright © 2011 GRIN Verlag, Open Publishing GmbH
Print and binding: Books on Demand GmbH, Norderstedt Germany
ISBN: 978-3-668-14203-9

**This book at GRIN:**

http://www.grin.com/en/e-book/315182/the-third-way-positive-welfare-the-schroeder-blair-paper-and-criticism

**Anonym**

**The "Third Way". Positive Welfare, the Schröder-Blair-Paper and Criticism of the Concept**

GRIN Publishing

**GRIN - Your knowledge has value**

Since its foundation in 1998, GRIN has specialized in publishing academic texts by students, college teachers and other academics as e-book and printed book. The website www.grin.com is an ideal platform for presenting term papers, final papers, scientific essays, dissertations and specialist books.

**Visit us on the internet:**

http://www.grin.com/

http://www.facebook.com/grincom

http://www.twitter.com/grin_com

Philipps-Universität Marburg
Fachbereich 03 – Gesellschaftswissenschaften und Philosophie
Institut für Politikwissenschaft
Wintersemester 2011/2012
SE Welfare State Research: An Introduction
Datum: 13.12.2011

# The Third Way

## Structure

1. Positive Welfare (Anthony Giddens)

2. The Schröder-Blair-Paper

3. Criticism (Barkan, Butterwegge)

4. Discussion

References

# 1.          Positive Welfare

**Anthony Giddens**
- advisor of Tony Blair
- author of „The Third Way"

**Positive Welfare**
- the state must provide a basic income
- state supports self-responsibility
- increasing benefits can cause moral hazard→ changed social habits

→social investment state instead of welfare state

# 2.          The Schröder-Blair-Paper

**Introduction**
- modernization of Social Democrats led to political success
→ market economy but not a market society

**Learning from Experience**
- social justice ≠ equality of outcome
- helping people to help themselves is more important than public spending
→ the weaknesses of markets have been overstated and their strengths underestimated

# 2.      The Schröder-Blair-Paper

**New Programs for Changed Realities**
- useless of left-right thinking
- ideology = preconceptions which prevent pragmatic solutions
- investments in human capital
- jobs are limited in time → more flexibility necessary
- cutbacks and reformations in the public sector
- end of the conflict between capital and labour

# 2.      The Schröder-Blair-Paper

**A New Supply-Side Agenda for the Left**
- creation of jobs → guarantee of a cohesive society -
liberalization of world trade
- taxcuts for companies
- welfare-to-work programs
- reduction of non-wage labour costs
- flexibilisation of products, capital and labour markets
- lifelong education
- support of medium-sized enterprises

# 2.      The Schröder-Blair-Paper

**An Active Labour Market Policy for the Left**
- transformation of the safety net of entitlements into a springboard to personal responsibility
- modernization of the health care and pension system - qualifications for the unemployed
- part-time and low-paid work
- establishment of a low-wage sector

# 3.      Criticism (Barkan, Butterwegge)

- left-right-thinking makes sense
- (some) equality of outcome is implied by social justice
- lots of empty phrases / missing characterizations
- jobs might be limited
- no words about people's rights
- compulsion to work
- not clear how the conception will be financed
- destroys the solidarity between the working and the unemployed
- some members of society aren't able to help themselves
- unequal treatment of capital and labour

# 4.    Discussion

**Group 1**
  - Can you think of other points of critique looking back at „Third Way"
  Politics more than 10 years later?
  - How did „Third Way"Politics change the German welfare state?

**Group 2**
  - Is the „Third Way" a plan to dismantle the welfare state? - Is
  the „Third Way" a neoliberal agenda? Why (not)?

# References

- Giddens, Anthony (2006) [1998]: Positive Welfare. In: Pierson, Paul/Castles, Francis G. (Eds.): The Welfare State Reader (2nd Edition). Cambridge, U.K./Malden, M.A.: Polity Press, 378-388.

  - Blair, Tony/Schröder, Gerhard (2000) [1999]: Europe: The Third Way /
  Die Neue Mitte. Annotated by Joanne Barkan. In: Dissent, Spring 2000,
                          51-65.
- Butterwegge, Christoph (2006): Krise und Zukunft des
Sozialstaates. Wiesbaden 2005, 233-265.

**The Third Way**

## 0. Einleitung + Gliederung

- I welcome you to today's topic "The Third Way" respectively "Neue Mitte"
- The Social Democracy has changed a lot during the 1990s in Germany
    - especially under the Schröder-administration
- Their English counterpart, the Labour Party, did the same under the administration of Tony Blair
    - where the last marxist claims were discarded and the establishment of a so called New Labour took place
- The catchwords "Third Way" in England and "Neue Mitte" in Germany label this transition
- In 1999 the party members and voters were prepared to this transition with a document called "Europe: The Third Way" in England and "Der Weg nach vorne für Europas Sozialdemokraten" in Germany
    - the document is better known as the Schröder-Blair-paper, which contains a draft of modernization for the European Social Democracy

- In the following I want to present the main points of this concept and the criticism

    - Therefore I will present the concept of "Positive Welfare" by Anthony Giddens who is the main ideologue of New Labour (1)
    - Then I will show the main points of the Schröder-Blair-Paper in order (2)
    - to criticize it with the socialist Joanne Barkan and the poverty researcher Christoph Butterwegge(3)
    - In that case it would be interesting to discuss whether you agree with the critics or not (4)

## 1. Positive Welfare (Anthony Giddens)

- Anthony Giddens is the main ideologue of the "Third Way" between laissez-faire liberalism and socialism and he was an advisor of Tony Blair
- Positive Welfare is a dissociation of welfare-conceptions which contain insurance and security from things
    - like disease, unemployment, poverty and so on
    - Giddens prefers a welfare-conception which contains capabilities to do something
    - so the task of government is different, it provides the people with basic skills from which they can reach employment, health and so on in self-responsibility
-He argues that the difficulties of the welfare state are only partly financial
    - welfare states spent more on money social issues but the same time high unemployment, a growth in the numbers of in-work poor and changes in demographic patterns were underlying these efforts
- These increasing benefits can cause a moral hazard, according to Giddens
    - that means people who are getting used to social benefits will not work if these benefits are too high
    - so he fears a changed social habitus with
        - an increased tendency to apply for social assistance
        - more absence from work for alleged health reasons
        - and a lower level of job search

» Therefore he supports an effective risk management, where an investment in human capital takes place wherever possible in order to allow people founding their own businesses or taking a job

- the social investment state should be put in place of the welfare state
- that implies a return after the investment

» In his essay "Positive Welfare" he gave two examples of social investment strategies: provision for old age and unemployment

» In case of ageing he argues that it presents at least as many opportunities as problems for the individuals as well as the society

- the label pensioner is an invention of the welfare state and leads to a loss of self-esteem
- therefore the fixed age of retirement should be abolished
- people should be able to use their funds as they wish
- so they can finance education or reduced working hours when they need and not after reaching an specific age
- he concludes that the old age shouldn't be seen as a time of rights without responsibilities

» In case of unemployment he agrees with the businnes analyst Moss Kanter who identified five main areas where government policy can assist job creation

- It should support entrepreneurial initiatives concerned with small business startups and technological innovation
- a lifelong education
- private public partnerships to combine the resources of the public sector with private efficiency
- an enhanced portability through common standards of education or pension rights
- and finally family-friendly workplace policies which could be achieved by public-private collaborations

- Positive welfare is just a little part of Giddens Third Way vision

- globalization, individualism and environmental issues take a big role in his conception of the Third Way
- as well as the outdated thinking in Left-Right-categories

» His book "The Third Way" has the subtitle "The Renewal of Social Democracy" so it's clear who the ideas are addressed to

» I would take now a look at the Schröder-Blair-Paper which Giddens had enormous influence on if you don't have questions so far

## 2. The Schröder-Blair-Paper

- The Schröder-Blair-Paper was published in 1999

    - it was written by Bodo Hombach, former Federal Minister of the Chancellery and Peter Mandelson, an advisor of Tony Blair

        - both were supporters of a new direction in Social Democracy apart from socialist positions before


- The first point made in the **introduction** of the paper is that the success of Social Democrats all over Europe is a result of their modernization

    - Modernization in this context means that Social Demorcrats discovered economic dynamism besides the question of social justice
- Based on the paper, this modernization has to go on and contains a complementation and improving of the markets by political actions

    - so there is a clear commitment to market economy but not as they say to market society

        - the difference between both is unfortunately not explained


- The **first chapter**, headed "Learning from Experience" contains several mistakes which the Social Democrats made, according to Hombach and Mandelson

    - They argue social justice doesn't mean the imposition of equality of outcome
    - and it shouldn't be identified with higher levels of public spending

        - because that doesn't show how much it enables people to help themselves
    - The values which according to the paper are important to citizens like personal achievement and success, entrepreneurial spirit and individual responsibility were subordinated to universal social safeguards
    - The claim of more individual responsibility goes on in the paper and summarizes the first chapter by the sentence: "The weaknesses of markets have been overstated and their strengths underestimated."
    - the segregation of public spending and social justice fits completely with Giddens argumentation

        - and so does emphasize of personal responsibility
- The **second part** tries to show the problems of left-right categorizations in order to present the Social Democrats as the "Third Way" or "Neue Mitte"

    - They argue ideology means preconceptions and therefore it prevents practical solutions to problems
    - also money should be invested in "human capital" in order to enable people to help themselves to deal with new circumstances
    - The paper claims more flexibility from people because having a job for life is a thing of the past
    - environmental challenges shall be faced with a modern market-based approach and the concepts of efficiency
    - competition and high performance shall be promoted in the public sector where also cutbacks are claimed
    - At the end a spirit of community and solidarity is also claimed in the industrial relations

        - a partnership which overcomes the conflict between capital and labour shall be reached
    - so the argumentation is that these claims has nothing to do with left-right categories

The **next part** introduces the "New Supply-Side Agenda" for the Left

- which is quite confusing because one chapter earlier it was said the left-right thinking is not useful
- however the creation of jobs is pointed out as the guarantee of a cohesive society
- Caused by the high unemployment in the European Union a new supply-side agenda must be formulated
    - they also name what have to be done for that
        - a market framework, containing the EU continuing acting as a resolute force for liberalization of world trade and strengthening an economic framework conducive to productivity growth
        - a tax policy to promote sustainable growth
            - for example cutting corporate tax to raise the profitability and strengthen the incentives to invest
            - but also the taxation of work should be reduced
            - and taxation shall also depend on environmental-friendly behavior
        - The next point is the connection of demand and supply-side which contains several claims with positive effects on both sides like
            - Successful welfare-to-work programs with raising income and raising workers-supply
            - the reduction of non-wage labor costs which raise the income and makes labour cheap
            - an employment friendly taxation
            - deregulation of companies
            - and flexibilisation of products, capital and labor markets
        - Generally the document emphasizes the transition of economy from industrial production to knowledge-based service economy and a changed consumer-behavior
            - the suggested reactions are deregulation and flexibilisation
        - then a whole subchapter refers to the importance of education, as basis of flexibility
        - the medium-sized enterprises are identified as the biggest potential for growth and jobs
            - these enterprises need easier access to the capital markets
            - and deregulation as well as non-wage labour costs reduction will make it easier for individuals to set up businesses
        - the last subchapter refers to debts but doesn't contain any actions which need to be taken besides the statement that deficit spending is not the best answer
- Giddens influence can be seen here especially by the emphasis of education and flexibilisation

- The **fourth part** introduces the active labor market policy
    - which contains the transformation of quote "the safety net of entitlements into a springboard to personal responsibility"
    - This part of the Schröder-Blair-Paper is all about taking the state out of and the individual in responsibility
        - that means changes in the pension and health care system
        - Qualifications, part-time and low-paid work in cases of unemployment
        - Lowering non-wage labor costs
        - checking whether disabled people are really disabled
        - Establishment of a low-wage sector for low-skilled people
    - This is the main consequences of Giddens positive welfare
- The **fifth part** doesn't bring up any new so I ignored it


- Questions?


## 3. Criticism (Barkan, Butterwegge)
- Barkan and Butterwegge criticized several points directly referring to the paper
- One of the first protest concern the so called dogmas of left and right
    - Barkan and Butterwegge speak for retention of the terms because there is an identification with social justice from the left and with free markets from the right
-Barkan argues that social justice implies at least some degree of equality of outcome because they undermine future opportunities
    - Butterwegge disagrees also but goes a bit further
    - according to him there can't be an equality of opportunity if the unequal distribution of property and wealth aren't abolished
- Barkan in general criticizes the use of empty phrases especially when it comes on crime and drug issues and the lack of definitions and characterizations in terms like globalization, flexibility and so on
- The focus on education and training of people also doesn't necessarily create jobs
- According to Barkan it's also more important that the European Union guarantees labor rights, human rights and environmental protection instead of liberalization of world trade
    - Butterwegge argues the same way, when saying the Schröder-Blair-Paper is based on a model of duties for people in need and not a model of confident citizens who claim their rights
        - the social policy reprobates to a business-contract where supported people are in debt
        - compulsion to work is the logical consequence (like 1 Euro-jobs)
- Barkman indicates the high amout of money needed for education and lowering taxations and the paper doesn't say how that will be financed
- According to Butterwege the transformation of quote "the safety net of entitlements into a springboard to personal responsibility" fits perfect because it's just useful for the healthy and capable people
- He argues that the active labor market policy is the end of the welfare state under the masque of modernization
    - because it destroys the solidarity between working and unemployed people

- Also words like human capital, self-responsibility and private initiative would just conceal social irresponsibility of the state

    - because they imply that every member of society is able to help her or himself

    - meanwhile high earner and companies are supported without being determined to support society in a comparable way

# YOUR KNOWLEDGE HAS VALUE